By Laura Williams
Translated by Emi Takahashi

© 2022 Williams Books
1 rue de l'église, 91430 Igny
Dépôt légal : Décembre 2022
ISBN 978-2-494614-41-3
Imprimé à la demande par Amazon
Loi n° 49-956 du 16 juillet 1949 sur les publications destinées à la jeunesse

アンテロープ
[antelope] – antelope

バット
[batto] – bat

クマ
[kuma] – bear

トコジラミ
[tokojirami] – bedbug

蜂
[hachi] – bee

バッファロー
[baffaro] – buffalo

蝶々
[chocho] – butterfly

ラクダ
[rakuda] – camel

猫
[neko] – cat

カメレオン
[kamereon] – chameleon

ひよこ

[hiyoko] – chick

鶏

[tori] – chicken

ゴキブリ

[gokiburi] – cockroach

牛

[ushi] – cow

クリケット

[kuriketto] – cricket

クロコダイル

[kurokodairu] – crocodile

犬

[inu] – dog

ロバ

[roba] – donkey

アヒル
[ahiru] – duck

ミミズ
[mimizu] – earthworm

ゾウ

[zou] – elephant

魚

[sakana] – fish

ハエ
[hae] – fly

キツネ
[kitsune] – fox

カエル
[kaeru] – frog

ガゼル
[gazeru] – gazelle

キリン
[kirin] – giraffe

ヤギ
[yagi] – goat

ガチョウ
[gacho] – goose

カバ
[kaba] – hipopotamus

馬
[uma] – horse

ハイエナ
[haiena] – hyena

ライオン
[raion] – lion

トカゲ
[tokage] – lizard

モグラ
[mogura] – mole

マングース
[mangusu] – mongoose

猿
[saru] – monkey

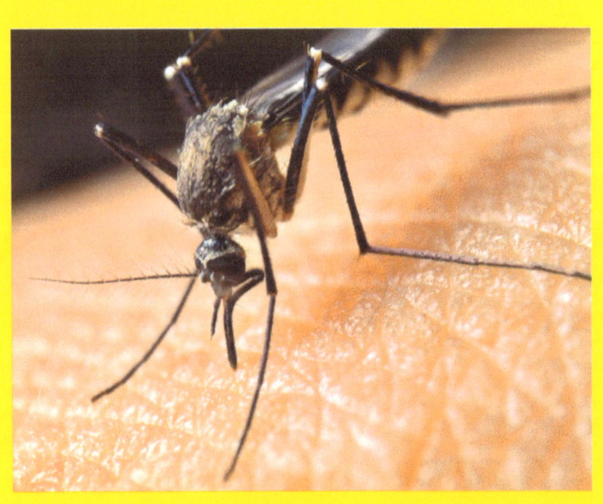

蚊
[hae] – mosquito

ネズミ
[nezumi] – mouse

オウム
[oumu] – parrot

豚

[buta] – pig

ハト

[hato] – pigeon

ウサギ
[usagi] – rabbit

雄鶏
[osudori] – rooster

羊
[hitsuji] – sheep

カタツムリ
[katatsumuri] – snail

蛇

[hebi] – snake

クモ

[kumo] – spider

カリバチ
[karibachi] – wasp

シマウマ
[shimauma] – zebra

Thank you

Thank you for purchasing "Japanese-English Words for Toddlers"! Your support means a lot to me, and I hope you and your child enjoy these books.

If you have a moment, I would greatly appreciate it if you could leave a review on Amazon. Your feedback will help me improve future editions of the series and create more resources for bilingual children.

Thank you again for your support. You can access the reviews on Amazon by scanning the QR code below or by visiting the link below:

https://www.amazon.com/review/create-review?&asin=2494614414

Thank you for helping me continue my work as a language teacher and translator. Your support is greatly appreciated!

In the same collection

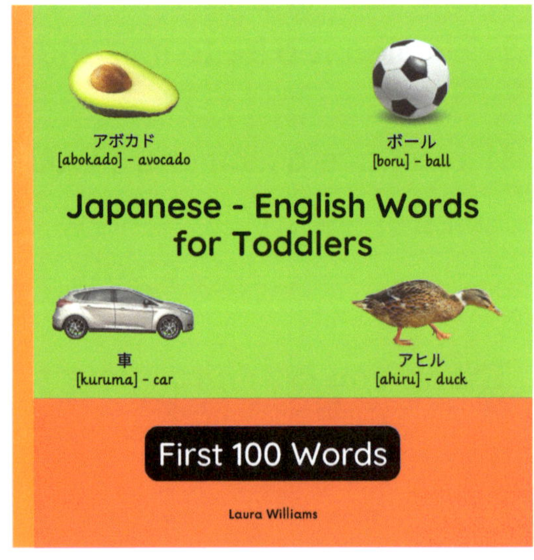